SCRAMBLED
HORMONES
60 Days of Encouragement for Moms
Raising Teenage Daughters

SCRAMBLED
HORMONES
60 Days of Encouragement for Moms
Raising Teenage Daughters

by

MONICA CANE

WordCrafts

Scrambled Hormones
    60 Days of Encouragement for Moms Raising Teenage Daughters
Copyright © 2014
Monica Cane

Cover photography & design by David Warren

Published by WordCrafts Press
Tullahoma, TN 37388
www.wordcrafts.net

This book is dedicated to all moms raising teenage daughters.

It may not always seem like it,
but your daughter really does hear you,
really does need you,
and really does love you.

Don't give up.
Keep praying.
Keep believing.

Contents

Introduction

I imagine any woman who happens to come across this book and reads the title, ***Scrambled Hormones***, is going to want to grab it with both hands, clutch it to her chest and let out a deep sigh of relief, grateful that someone understands that as women our hormones are indeed scrambled.

One minute we are up, they next we are down. One moment we believe we are more than conquers, the next moment we believe we are insignificant grasshoppers. One day we feel loved, well balanced and happy, the next day we feel alone, out of control and unworthy. It's a crazy cycle, one that seems to begin just shy of the teenage years and picks up full speed for many years to follow. We eventually have teenagers of our own and just when we think we've got the hormone thing licked for ourselves, something ridiculous called pre-menopause hits us and we spiral out of hormonal control all over again. Suddenly mother and daughter find themselves in a hormone blizzard.

I remember vividly as a teenager when the hormone thing kicked in for me. I suddenly felt angry, emotional and out of control on a regular basis but I didn't quite know why. Like most teenagers, I was certain at the time that my irrational behavior was my parents' fault. I willingly played the blame game and gave my parents grief, particularly my mom, as my fluctuating hormones reached tsunami proportions. I remember thinking that things would be so much different when I had teenagers of my own. I believed I would somehow help them breeze through the teen years, "hormone-problem free," and they would be ever so grateful. Boy, was I wrong.

I have two beautiful, good-natured, kind-hearted, adult daughters whom I love with all my heart, but oh those teen years were some tough times. Between their irrational teen hormones and my pre-menopausal ones - well, we all but drove each other crazy.

When I began considering what kind of book I wanted to write, I instantly thought back to that season of my life when I was raising my teenage daughters, and how often I needed encouragement, guidance and overall hope that I wasn't losing my mind, especially whenever the hormones and attitudes flew out of control.

Reflecting back to all that God had shown me during that hormonal season and how faithful He was, I just knew I had to share some of that hope with other moms.

Scrambled Hormones: 60 Days of Encouragement for Moms Raising Teenage Daughters, shares 60 devotionals combining scriptures with personal experiences to encourage your faith during the scrambled-hormone-teenage-raising season. Each devotion concludes with:

The Problem: real struggles we have as moms (and as women).

The Promise: a reminder of God's truth based on His Word.

The Plan: thoughts, tips or activities to strengthen mom's heart and soul.

My prayer is that as you read this book, you will see from my examples that as moms we are not perfect, but we do serve a perfect God who not only loves us but fully understands our scrambled hormones and will gladly help us grow as mothers, daughters and women through them.

Comfort, *transitive verb*
    : To give strength and hope to
    : To ease the grief or trouble of

Apples of Gold

The right word spoken at the right time is as beautiful as gold apples in a silver bowl.

Proverbs 25:11

When children are small, most moms try to teach them the importance of saying nice things. Many little ones have heard the mom speech, "If you can't say something nice, don't say anything at all," and have been mindful to heed Mama's words.

Strange how things can change when the teen years hit. For one reason or another, harsh words that would have never been considered in the younger years are now voiced in the heat of the moment by both parent and teen.

During my youngest daughter's teen years I found myself so frustrated that, at times, I would say hurtful things. I love my daughter with all my heart, but some days the hormones and teen drama made me crazy, and I would spew out words of anger that I never meant to say. By the time she turned eighteen and had moved out to volunteer with a ministry, a number of unkind words had been spouted between us.

One afternoon my daughter called me, and to our mutual delight we had the most healing of conversations. It wasn't filled with many words; as a matter of fact, there was a lot of silence between us. But because God had been softening my heart - and apparently my daughter's as well - I took the first step to say that I was sorry for not always being the best example of a Christian. Just a few simple words expressing a sincere apology were apples of gold to my daughter. She in turn apologized, and I found apples of gold as well.

The Problem: In my anger I have said hurtful words.

The Promise: The right word spoken at the right time is as beautiful as gold apples in a silver bowl.

The Plan: Learn to say "I'm sorry" quickly and often, and enjoy the apples of gold.

Can You Relate?

Encourage each other and give each other strength.

1 Thessalonians 5:11

As I began writing this book I had the wonderful idea to add a few personal stories from a few moms who had already been through the teen years with their daughters and had experienced God's comforting hand during that time.

As soon as I got the thumbs-up from the publisher I sent out an email asking moms with now-grown daughters if they would like to share a mother/teen daughter testimony. While waiting for their response, the craziest thought crossed my mind. For one very brief moment I thought, *What if the moms I emailed couldn't relate? What if I was the only mom who experienced teen drama and scrambled hormones?*

It took just a moment for that ridiculous thought to enter my mind before I began laughing out loud. Of course the moms I emailed could relate. Just about every mom who has ever raised a teen daughter could relate, and that's why I felt inclined to write a book that would encourage them during their time of need.

One of my dearest friends, although having no children yet, was able to fully understand and relate through other means to the mother/daughter scrambled hormones issues. She was my biggest supporter emotionally and spiritually during that season. She was the one who always reminded me to take care of myself first so that I could take better care of my teenagers along with the rest of my family. God gave me this friend at just the right time. A friend who could understand in her own way and who strengthened me with her unconditional love and encouragement.

The Problem: I need encouragement.

The Promise: Encourage each other, and give each other strength.

The Plan: As you receive encouragement make sure to pay it forward.

God Is Our Resource

No matter how many promises God has made,
they are 'Yes' in Christ.

2 Corinthians 1:20

Recently I was perusing the bookshelves at my local Christian bookstore for a devotional booklet to give to my oldest daughter and her husband for Christmas, when I stumbled upon the book, *Have a New Teenager by Friday,* written by Dr. Kevin Leman.

I could have used a book like that, one that helps parents gain respect from their teenager, establish healthy boundaries, communicate with the "whatever" generation, turn selfish behavior around, navigate the critical years with confidence and prepare their teen for life now and in the future. But I was so heavily focused on all the teen drama at the time I didn't even realize this particular resource was available. I did however, make a point to glean from some helpful parenting resources in addition to receiving godly counsel while continually looking to God for answers.

I did everything I knew to do, and while I never had a "new teenager by Friday," I was able to recognize God working and moving within both of my girls.

No doubt I would have devoured a book like Dr. Leman's, and perhaps it would have helped me navigate my way through the hormone stage a bit better. But even if I had been able to add his book to my repertoire of parental help books, and even if I had applied all the principles he suggests, as a Christian mom I still would have to come to the place of needing to trust the promises of God.

The Problem: I need resources I can count on.

The Promise: No matter how many promises God has made, they are "Yes" in Christ.

The Plan: The promises of God will always be your greatest resource, but occasionally it helps to have outside resources and godly counsel.

His Comforting Protection

*Those who go to God Most High for safety will
be protected by the Almighty.*

Psalm 91:1

Psalm 91:1 is one of those verses that always manages
to show up at just the right time. I first read it when
my girls were little and I had come down with what
I thought was the flu. My head was spinning and my
stomach had been doing summersaults for days.
Eventually visiting my doctor, I learned that it wasn't the
flu but an inner ear ailment similar to vertigo, called
labyrinthitis, which was usually brought on by a viral or
bacterial infection.

My doctor assured me that it would go away within
two to four weeks, but added a caveat - in some rare cases
it lasted longer. Unfortunately, I was one of those rare
cases. I suffered from labrynthitis for four months. While
it wasn't a life-threatening disease, because it affected my
equilibrium I began to experience a lot of fear and
anxiety. That's when God first revealed the promise of
Psalm 91:1. I went to Him for safety and found great
comfort and a sense of His protection over all my fears.

Years later when my girls hit the teenage years, when kids seem to believe they are invincible, my fears and anxiety returned, this time throwing my emotional equilibrium into a tizzy.

God in His faithfulness brought Psalm 91:1 to my attention again, reminding me that while the situation was different, His promises of protection for those who look to Him for safety were the same.

The Problem: I need to feel safe and protected, again.

The Promise: Those who go to God Most High for safety will be protected by the Almighty.

The Plan: Stop whatever you are doing and consider this question: "Is there anything at all that God cannot protect you or your loved ones from?"

Pass the Comfort

He comforts us every time we have trouble, so when others have trouble, we can comfort them with the same comfort God gives us.

2 Corinthians 1:4

Every author has a reason for writing the books that he or she writes. My reason for writing this book was because I couldn't seem to get away from the memories of needing comfort during the season of raising teenage girls. I'm not implying that every waking moment of the teen years was a nightmare, because it wasn't. There were many special mother/daughter moments shared during those years, but if you're a mom raising emotionally charged girls then you know the struggle is real.

One of the hardest lessons for me to learn as a mom during the teen years was to take a step back from all the hormonal chaos, from the bickering and the fix-it-Mama-mode, and to simply focus on taking care of myself physically, mentally, spiritually and emotionally. It was not easy, and I needed many reminders. But whenever I did step back, whenever I did take better care of myself, that's when I was able to receive the most comfort from God.

I found comfort and courage in His Word and in prayer during that season. I hope to pass some of that same comfort and courage on to you. If you are in the hormonal teen-rearing season, take care of yourself by drawing near to God.

The Problem: I need comfort.

The Promise: He comforts us every time we have trouble, so when others have trouble, we can comfort them.

The Plan: Make yourself a plate of healthy comfort food today, such as Greek yogurt blueberry pancakes (www.notyouraveragecollegefood.com).

While you sit and enjoy this delicious comfort food, remind yourself that God is your Comforter. Feel free to share a plate of healthy comfort food with a friend.

We Change, but God Doesn't

Jesus Christ is the same yesterday, today and forever.

Hebrews 13:8

When my oldest daughter was in third grade, she came home one afternoon and told me how she had the opportunity to share a scripture with another little girl in her class who had been worried about many things. My little girl beamed with pride and sincere happiness as she re-told the events leading up to sharing the Word of God with her classmate. I felt like the proudest mom ever as I saw the genuineness in her eyes. At nine years old she had a heart for ministry. All she wanted was for others to know the love of Jesus just like she did.

Years later as she prepared to enter high school, typically known as the most tumultuous time in a teenage girl's life, I wondered if her sincere, God-fearing, people-loving nature would still be there by the time graduation rolled around, or if she would get lost along the way. I worried that her tender heart might become jaded by experiences such as unwelcoming cliques and pettiness, or the hormonal surges that can affect a young girl's self-image.

Although I wasn't certain how things might change for my teenage daughter throughout high school and as she grew into adulthood, one thing I was certain of was this truth: *"Jesus Christ is the same yesterday, today and forever."*

Change can be scary, but look at it this way: Without it we wouldn't be the moms that we are now, and our girls wouldn't grow into the women they're meant to be. While my daughter did indeed go through changes, Jesus remained the same and so did her love for Him and for others.

The Problem: Change is scary.

The Promise: Jesus Christ is the same yesterday, today, and forever.

The Plan: Reflect on this acronym:

Courageous
Hope
Affects
New
Grace
Everyday

Healing, *transitive verb*
　　: To make sound or whole
　　: To restore to health

Be Your Own Cheerleader

*I am like an olive tree flourishing in the house
of God's unfailing love.*

Psalm 52:8

Moms are great cheerleaders. A mom's child could come in dead last in a school race, but that mom would still be cheering her child on from the sidelines and shouting with joy as if her child was about to win a gold medal in the Olympics.

Even the turbulent teen years can't stop the cheerleader in moms, as they are known to leave encouraging notes on pillows, in lunch bags or sent via text saying things like:

*You can do all things in Christ who strengthens
you. Have a great day.*

Love, Mom.

But even that mom who is the ultimate cheerleader, who can encourage the socks off of her kids - even the crazy, rebellious teenage ones - often needs that same encouragement she offers others for herself.

I don't know one mom who wouldn't love it if her kids, especially during the teen years, cheered her on, encouraged her and helped to strengthen her spirit the way she does for them. While some teens actually do just that, most are too focused on trying to figure out what in the world is going on within their own complicated lives to become Mom's cheerleader.

For this very reason, moms need to fellowship with one another for support and comfort, to remind each other to cheer for themselves just as much as they do for others. There is nothing like having another mama remind you that you can do all things through Christ who strengthens you, because you are meant to flourish too.

The Problem: I cheer for everyone but myself.

The Promise: *I am like an olive tree flourishing in the house of God's unfailing love.*

The Plan: Create a cheer list to remind yourself that you are an amazing mom and are designed to flourish in God's love.

God of Hope, Joy and Peace

*God who gives hope will fill you with much joy
and peace while you trust in him. Then your
hope will overflow by the power of the Holy
Spirit.*

Romans 15:13

This morning I was reading from a list of scriptural
declarations that a dear friend of mine emailed to
me yesterday. I recognized those declarations
(confessions) as a foundation to help build my faith, and
as a reminder of the power we have in speaking God's
truth over our lives.

As I read through the list of confessions that were re-
worded in a personal manner to make them more
applicable, my emotions began stirring more and more
with each one. By the time I read the confession based on
the truth of Romans 15:13, which says, *"I expect the best
day of my life spiritually, emotionally, relationally and
financially in Jesus name,"* I was a blubbering fool.

I couldn't stop crying as I thought about how many
times I had shared Romans 15:13 with a hurting mama
who needed the reminder that God wants to give us hope,

joy and peace every day, yet I would often forget to declare that same truth for myself.

I considered how differently I could have dealt with various situations, including the scrambled hormone years, had I made this declaration of scriptural truth over my life each and every day during that time. Although the scrambled hormones have passed, my need for this confession hasn't. I can begin today, and so can you.

The Problem: I don't always apply what I believe.

The Promise: God who gives hope will fill you with much joy and peace while you trust in Him. Then your hope will overflow by the power of the Holy Spirit.

The Plan: Begin declaring the truth of Romans 15:13 over yourself regularly:

"I expect the best day of my life spiritually, emotionally, relationally and financially in Jesus name."

God the Encourager

*The Lord your God is with you, the mighty One
will save you. He will rejoice over you. You will
rest in his love; He will sing and be joyful about
you.*

Zephaniah 3:17

This morning I was praying for you. Yes you, the one reading this devotion right now. Sitting in my favorite hideaway spot - my walk-in closet - I imagined you in the midst of parenting your teenage daughter, needing just a bit of encouragement.

Even if today is a great day for you, filled with wonderful experiences, a joyful, hormonally balanced day for both mother and daughter, I know from my own experience as the mama, that you can always use a little more encouragement. As I prayed for you, I asked the Lord to show me how I could encourage you best. Before I finished praying, Zephaniah 3:17 came to mind. Through it, this is what I believe God wants you, sweet mom, to know.

The Lord your God is with you. – *I am with you each and every day, I will not leave you, not even for a moment.*

The mighty One will save you. *– I saved you for eternity when you gave your life to Me. But I also am here to save you anytime you feel overwhelmed, tired and afraid.*

He will rejoice over you. *– I rejoice over you because you are My beautiful daughter.*

You will rest in His love. *– I love you unconditionally, and you can find rest in Me.*

He will sing and be joyful about you. *– I sing and am joyful about you because I am proud of who you are and who you will become.*

The Problem: I need encouragement, again.

The Promise: The Lord your God is with you.

The Plan: When you need encouragement, look to God's Word. Personalize the scriptures and know He is speaking encouragement to you.

L.O.L. = Laugh Out Loud

The one who sits in heaven laughs.

Psalm 2:4

I f you happen to be one of those moms who have been fortunate enough to only see the good side of teenage life then feel free to skip right past this devotion. But for the rest of us moms who have experienced the good, the bad and the oh-so-ugly side of raising teens, stay right here.

One of the real eye-openers I had while raising my teenage daughters was realizing that every problem wasn't just due to hormonal changes, but that there was also a very real spiritual battle going on inside of them.

Both girls had given their hearts to Jesus when they were young, and they truly loved the Lord. But during their teen years Satan kicked it up a notch and attempted to do just as John 10:10 reveals - steal, kill and destroy the confidence, self-esteem and faith of both girls. Satan couldn't have their soul, but he sure could wreak havoc on their belief system, which in turn wreaked havoc on mine.

While there were various factors as to why there was so much turbulence during my daughters' teen years, through much prayer, Scripture and godly counsel I began to understand that the enemy was nothing but trouble. He sought every opportunity to attack our weak areas, including the hormonal ones.

Psalm 2:2-4 tells of the enemy making plans to fight against the Lord and His appointed ones. But what was God's response? He laughed. He didn't take the enemy's threat seriously because He knew His will would prevail.

Though the enemy can fight dirty during the teen years, he doesn't win. We can laugh in the face of our enemy and trust God.

The Problem: Sometimes things can get ugly.

The Promise: The One who sits in heaven laughs.

The Plan: If God can laugh in the face of our enemy, what do we really have to fear?

Strive for Excellence, Not Perfection

Make every effort to respond to God's promises. Supplement your faith with a generous provision of moral excellence, and moral excellence with knowledge.

2 Peter 1:5 (NLT)

We live in a culture that promotes perfectionism. On a daily basis we are bombarded with the idea of achieving success through being the perfect size, owning the perfect house or driving the perfect car. Being Christian moms makes us no less susceptible to the perfectionism pressure of our culture. As a matter of fact, Christian moms can regularly take perfectionism to a whole other level as we strive for perfect Christian families, marriages and ministries.

Interestingly, much of that striving for Christian perfectionism is what often sets off the emotional time bomb between a mother and daughter during the teen years. Typically, Mom has done her best to maintain a perfect environment for years, and then the ever-changing hormones kick in and attitudes change, blowing perfectionism out the window.

The irony of the whole "perfect" struggle is that God has never called moms, daughters or anyone else to be perfect, but simply to follow Him.

A quote by Edwin Bliss says it well. "The pursuit of excellence is gratifying and healthy. The pursuit of perfection is frustrating, neurotic and a terrible waste of time."

Moms, daughters and people in general are not perfect. We can try all we want, but we will fail in our pursuit of perfection. How much different relationships would be, including that of the mother/daughter relationship, if we stopped expecting perfection from others or perfection from ourselves. Instead of perfection we should strive to develop a Christ-like nature of excellence, one day at a time.

The Problem: I want to be perfect.

The Promise: Supplement your faith with a generous provision of moral excellence, and moral excellence with knowledge.

The Plan: Seek God for understanding as to where you may need to let go of perfectionism and begin pursuing His excellence.

You are Destined

*Whoever believes in me will do the same things
that I do.*

John 14:12

When my kids were young I had a clear vision for my destiny as a Christian mom. I understood my calling. But during the scrambled hormones season I lost that vision. I couldn't make out my destiny because I was too busy trying to put out my teenagers' and my own emotional fires.

I would love to tell you that I prayed once for clarity and the vision for my destiny immediately returned, but that wasn't the case. What did happen, however, was that I spent many days and nights hiding in my closet, praying, journaling, seeking and reading the Bible for assurance and direction.

The cloud of not understanding my personal destiny still hovered over me, but it was these spiritual practices done on a regular basis that kept me connected in my relationship with God. I whined, I complained, and in those moments when I allowed the truth of God's Word to wash over me just a little more than normal, I did sense a measure of peace. But I still didn't have the clarity of vision I once had.

There was no magical moment; it just took time well spent with God. Eventually, as the girls grew out of their hormonal outbursts and I grew out of mine, clarity regarding my destiny returned. As the cloud lifted, I was able to clearly see how spending that time seeking and relating to God through prayer and His Word, even when I didn't feel what I wanted to feel, was actually part of fulfilling my destiny as a mom and as a believer.

The Problem: I can't see my destiny.

The Promise: Whoever believes in Me will do the same things that I do.

The Plan: Read John 14. Remember, Jesus fulfilled His destiny, and He says you can do the same if you believe in Him.

Truth, *noun*
    : The quality or state of being true
    : A statement or idea that is true or accepted as true

A Change of Perspective

All your children will be taught by the Lord,
and they will have much peace.

Isaiah 54:13

Many times when a dear friend shares with me the challenges she's experienced with her teenager, I will ask, "Why didn't you call me?" My friend typically responds, "Oh, I don't know; I just felt so overwhelmed." I certainly understand that dilemma.

Often, during the scrambled hormones years, I just didn't know how to share what I was feeling with a friend. I felt too overwhelmed, so I kept to myself. One day God brought a new friend my way. We began talking and, before I knew it, I was unloading my mom struggles to her. I shared how raising girls during the teen years left me feeling pretty inadequate. I explained how I felt little peace in my house of hormones. My new friend listened and offered words of comfort, letting me know she understood.

A few days later she brought me a handmade gift, a magnet with the verse, Isaiah 54:13. When I read it I wondered, though it was incredibly kind of her to give me a gift, why that particular verse. Nothing that was going on at the time reflected the truth of this scripture, and for a brief moment the verse felt like salt in a wound. Nevertheless, I appreciated the gift and put it on my nightstand, reading it daily.

Circumstances didn't instantly change, but as I continued to read the verse I found that my perspective on the situation did. Isaiah 54:13 became a promise from God that I could stand on. He would teach my daughters as He was teaching me, and He would bring the peace.

The Problem: I don't have the answer.

The Promise: All your children will be taught by the Lord, and they will have much peace.

The Plan: Write out Isaiah 54:13.

Do the Right Thing

Those who suffer as God wants should trust their souls to the faithful Creator as they continue to do what is right.

1 Peter 4:19

Early on I taught my girls the importance of always doing the right thing and being people of integrity, and how by doing so it brings honor to God. They took my word for it and did their best to be little girls of honor. Later, when puberty and peer influence took over, the idea of doing the right things in order to bring honor to God wasn't nearly as important as fitting in with the crowd.

I recall having many conversations with each daughter during the ages of thirteen to eighteen, encouraging them toward doing what was right in various situations, only to discover that my words had fallen on deaf ears. They were at that age when they thought I was too square, too strict and even too spiritual. Nevertheless, I continued to point both of my daughters toward God and His Word. As time went on, seeing each daughter follow the words of their peers more than the

Word of God, I began to wonder when or if doing the right thing as a Christian mom was going to pay off.

As frustrating as it felt at times, God kept bringing me back to what I needed to do. I was to continue to do what was right before my teenage daughters. Regardless of when it would pay off, being a mom of integrity for the long haul was the very example they needed.

The Problem: Doing the right thing is hard.

The Promise: Those who suffer as God wants should trust their souls to the faithful Creator as they continue to do what is right.

The Plan: Look up scriptures on integrity to remind yourself why it pays to do the right thing.

God Chose You Indeed

Before I made you in your mother's womb, I chose you.

Jeremiah 1:5

When my youngest daughter was born, though she was my third child, it was the very first time I actually realized that God *is* the Creator of life.

In my complete ignorance, I had basically given myself the credit for creating such beautiful kids the first two times. I didn't understand that I was merely a vessel and that it was God's creative design that formed my little beauties. It was when seeing my third red-faced, wrinkly, beautiful newborn that I finally had an epiphany - God creates life.

It's no wonder that upon committing my life to God a year after my daughter's birth, I was drawn to scriptures such as Jeremiah 1:5 - *"I knew you before I formed you in your mother's womb,"* and Psalm 139:15 - *"My frame was not hidden from you when I was made in the secret place."*

I believe God gave me the epiphany about Himself upon the birth of my second daughter - a spiritual marker that would forever remind me of His faithfulness, particularly during trying seasons, just as He did for the Israelites long ago.

It just so happened that my most trying season had to do with raising teenage daughters and learning how to maneuver through all the hormones. At the height of hormonal mother/teenage daughter tensions, when I thought perhaps I had fallen short one too many times as Mom and wondered if God was tired of caring, He would always remind me of that spiritual marker moment when I realized that He is our Creator. He will always love and care for His creation, even the hormonal ones.

The Problem: I'm not a perfect mom.

The Promise: Before I made you in your mother's womb, I chose you.

The Plan: Take a long look at yourself in the mirror then say aloud, "God chose me."

Speak Life

What you say can mean life or death. Those who speak with care will be rewarded.

Proverbs 18:21

When a mom tells her toddler, teen or adult child, "I believe in you; you can do it," it's easy to see just how much her positive words inspire her child. On the other hand, when mom is at her wits' end for one parental reason or another and shouts things like, "I brought you into this world, and I can take you out of it!" regardless of how ridiculous it sounds, the negative words can be disheartening.

While unkind words are tossed around from time to time between family members, for the most part, moms are the ones who readily have life-giving words on the tips of their tongues and are ready to offer encouragement when needed. For this very reason, despite all the madness that can take place between mother and daughters during hormone years - including the infamous "you're ruining my life" stage - as soon as the dust settles, Mom is still the one daughters tend to seek out for a life-giving word when needed.

Just as Mom holds the power to speak positive or negative words to her children, the friends who a mom surrounds herself with can hold the same kind of power over her.

During the trying teen years, I was careful to surround myself with friends who knew how to speak encouraging words over me and to me. The last thing a mom needs is words of discouragement when hormones have gone wild in her household. The life-giving words spoken to me by my friends helped me to continue speaking life-giving words to my children.

The Problem: Sometimes my tongue causes problems.

The Promise: Those who speak with care will be rewarded.

The Plan: Evaluate the friends you keep closest to you. Do they regularly speak life-giving words to you as friend, a woman and a mom?

The Truth about Discipline

The Lord disciplines those he loves, and he punishes everyone he accepts as his child.

Hebrews 12:6

I still remember what it felt like to discipline each of my children for the very first time. To go from kisses and hugs when they were babies to the need for stern correction for their own well-being as they grew wasn't easy.

By the time my girls hit their stride in the teen years I felt as if disciplining was the only language I spoke. There was always so much correction needed, as they were typical teenagers trying to spread their wings too fast, too soon.

Contrary to a teenager's belief that moms enjoy disciplining, moms know the truth. There is a constant tug-of-war that causes havoc on our emotions. We know that we are not always the favored parent, particularly during the emotional teen years when we're faced with the choice of standing our ground and disciplining more than expected. That can be a scary time for a mom who just wants to keep the little teenage chicks in her nest happy.

Looking to the Word of God for answers, we learn that God disciplines us because He loves us, knows what's best for us and wants to keep us on the right track so we can grow and be the best we were created to be. Isn't that what we want for our children as well?

No child likes discipline, and it only gets worse when the I-want-to-be-independent teen years hit. But hang in there Mom, and remember, discipline is evidence of love - God's love for us and your love for your child.

The Problem: Discipline makes me the bad guy.

The Promise: The Lord disciplines those He loves.

The Plan: Reflect on how God has disciplined you over the years. How could you tell it was done in love? What did you learn from it?

Unconditional. Believe It

Neither death, nor life, nor angels, nor ruling spirits, nothing now, nothing in the future, no powers, nothing above us, nothing below us, nor anything else in the whole world will ever be able to separate us from the love of God that is in Christ Jesus our Lord.

Romans 8:38-39

I considered the possibility of only using a portion of Romans 8:38-39 in this devotion, simply for the sake of keeping with the proper word count on each page. But the more I read the verses and considered which portion of it I should use, the more certain I became that this truth of God's unending, unstoppable, unconditional love needed to be shared in its entirety, regardless of the possibility of hogging up the word count.

If I wrote nothing else on this page but this scripture, it would be enough. I probably could say this about every Bible verse, but I honestly believe this particular scripture is one of the extra special ones. It's the crème de la crème in my opinion because of its undeniable answer to one of our deepest fears: *Have I messed up so much that God could stop loving me? Or leave me?*

Teenagers wonder about it. Moms wonder about it. As a matter fact, most everyone wonders about it at one point or another. Everyone needs reassurance of God's unconditional love, and through this verse He gives it. We are loved by God completely.

Sometimes when scrambled hormones kick in for mothers and daughters and friction picks up, the best thing you both can do is just stop where you are and take a moment to reflect on the unconditional love God has for you.

The Problem I've really blown it.

The Promise: Nothing in the whole world will ever be able to separate us from the love of God.

The Plan: Receive it and believe it.

Peace, *noun*
: A state of tranquility or quiet
: Harmony in personal relations

Scrambled Hormones

*You, Lord, give true peace to those who depend
on you, because they trust in you.*

Isaiah 26:3

I didn't understand what was happening. Why was my
once loving little girl turning into a destructive
tornado of unpredictable emotions? I had expected
hormonal challenges during her teen years, but this was
extreme. One moment she was happy, full of energy and
chatting a mile a minute about all the good things in life;
the next moment she was depressed, irritable and lashing
out in angry outbursts.

I did everything I knew to comfort and encourage
her, but nothing seemed to help. As the developing teen
years settled in and her extreme mood swings took over, I
found my own emotions unraveling. Before I knew it, I
was struggling with extreme mood swings of my own.

I realized I needed to restore a sense of peace in the
midst of the hormonal turbulence taking place in our
home. I knew from experience that the only way I could
restore any peace was by seeking help from God. Sitting
on the floor of my walk-in closet, I called on Him for

help. I wanted Him to remove the wave of problems in order to feel peace, but instead He showed me how to ride the wave with Him.

Life, similar to hormones, can hit full force like ocean waves crashing against the shore. While we hope the waves settle quickly, if we learn to lean on, trust in, and depend on Him through the waves, He will give us peace.

The Problem: I don't understand what's happening.

The Promise: You, Lord, give true peace to those who depend on you, because they trust in you.

The Plan: Commit Isaiah 26:3 to memory. Repeat it out loud daily as a reminder that God is trustworthy and will restore your peace.

Holy Spirit Junior, Part 1

But the Helper will teach you everything.

John 14:26

O ne morning I stopped by the church office to visit the wife of our then-pastor. I was pregnant and feeling, well, you guessed it, hormonal. She motioned for me to take a seat in a chair opposite her at her desk. I quickly settled into the seat, grateful for her listening ear, and then spent the next few minutes boo-hoo-ing over my expectations regarding the unity of family ministry.

I couldn't quite understand why my husband, our oldest daughter who was in her "tween" years, and I couldn't be on the same page regarding family ministry. I knew that we all loved the Lord with our whole hearts, but we each had very different approaches as to how we related to God and how we should best serve Him.

My pastor's wife listened patiently as I explained how much I dwelled on this issue and how I even offered godly hints regularly in hopes of helping my husband and tween to better understand the joy of serving God as a family.

When I finally took a breath between words, my pastor's wife graciously offered some sound advice.

"You're family may think that you are trying to be Pastor Monica. They may think you are trying to be Holy Spirit Junior." I was stunned at her words but knew deep down she was right. "Just step back and let God's Holy Spirit speak to their hearts," she concluded.

The Problem: Sometimes I take over the role of the Holy Spirit.

The Promise: But the Helper [The Holy Spirit] will teach you everything.

The Plan: To learn more about the role of the Holy Spirit, read John 16:7-11, Romans 8:9, and 1 Corinthians 6:19-20.

Holy Spirit Junior, Part 2

This Helper is the Holy Spirit.

John 14:26

My pastor's wife only had to tell me once, in her kind way, that I may have a tendency toward doing the Holy Spirit's job in the lives of my loved ones. Upon that wise counsel I went home, got on my knees and prayed.

I'm so sorry God for the times I have overstepped my boundary and tried to be You. I know sometimes I can go way beyond offering wise counsel and try to bring conviction, forgetting that conviction is Your job, not mine.

I was determined to leave the convicting to God from that moment on. And it worked too - that is until the teen years brought out a little bit of ugly in all of us. Bitter glares and lashing out phrases, such as, "You're ruining life," is only funny in movies like *Freaky Friday* starring Lindsey Lohan and Jamie Lee Curtis. In real life, it can be pretty upsetting.

As hormone-driven troubles escalated with my younger daughter, I once again found myself trying to be Holy Spirit Junior in her life. In truth, I believe as moms we all struggle a bit in this area because we just want the best for our children, even more so as they pass through the teen years and into adulthood.

The purpose of God's Holy Spirit dwelling in every believer is to convict, counsel, encourage and guide according to His will. While we as moms are called to encourage, guide and counsel as well, it's in a much different way than that of the Holy Spirit. The more I confronted that Holy Spirit Junior nature of mine, the easier it was to point my hormone-driven teenager to Jesus.

The Problem: I'm not the Holy Spirit.

The Promise: This Helper is the Holy Spirit.

The Plan: Do a study on the meaning of conviction versus condemnation.

I Choose Peace

You must choose for yourselves today whom you will serve.

Joshua 24:15

We were getting ready to downsize from our four-bedroom home to a quaint, but significantly smaller, two-bedroom duplex. As we began the moving process all I could think of was establishing some corner of our new little home as my own private place where I could go to regroup privately with God. I was emotionally exhausted from dealing with all the fluctuating teenage and pre-menopausal hormones that had been going on for some time, and I needed God-sized peace.

Setting the first moving box down in our new place, I found my God spot - a tiny patio with a faded white fence connecting our side of the duplex to our neighbor. After unpacking, the first thing I did was put a fresh coat of white paint on the fence. Then I used alphabet stencils to paint the words "I Choose Peace" in a chestnut brown right on the fence.

Adding a small table and chairs, I established the patio as my let-go-and-let-God space. I believe every woman can understand the need for a spot like this - particularly women who are raising teen girls and dealing with their changing moods and self-image struggles, not to mention the physical and emotional changes moms go through.

Joshua 24:15 speaks of choosing whom we are going to serve - God or the enemy. I came to realize in my peace patio that it also can apply to choosing how we respond to situations. Moms can choose things like love over anger, joy over sadness and peace over hormones every day. While it may not be easy, with God it is possible.

The Problem: I need to regroup.

The Promise: Choose for yourself today whom you will serve.

The Plan: Create a special spot for yourself. Fill it with reminders of the godly choices you want to make each day.

Let God Supply the Need

*God will supply all your needs according to the
riches of his glory in Christ Jesus.*

Philippians 4:19

I set my oven to 350 degrees and went about cracking
eggs, measuring sugar, sifting flour and combining
other ingredients in the mixing bowl to make the
perfect batch of cookies. Pouring the final ingredient into
the bowl - a bag of chocolate chunk chips - I glanced at
the oven to see if it was fully preheated.

I noticed a tiny red ember glowing through the
window of the oven door and went to take a closer look.
When I opened the oven door, the ember burst into a
flame that quickly burned its way around the wire at the
bottom of the oven before fizzling out and destroying it
completely.

I wanted to rush out and buy a new oven, but instead
I prayed and asked God to provide for our needs. I
quickly discovered that God already had provided, as
there were many electrical kitchen gadgets like a toaster
over, portable 2-burner stovetop, and a crock pot which
could easily replace an oven for the time being.

Trusting God to meet my oven needs reminded me of the many needs my daughters had as teenagers, and how I always rushed in to find a solution, often making matters worse instead of first asking God to supply their need.

It was a hard lesson to learn because daughters have your heart in away an oven never will. Nevertheless, just as with my oven, God often has the answer already in place and the need already met, but we won't see it until we stop trying to solve all the problems ourselves and start truly letting God meet our needs.

The Problem: I try to solve problems by myself.

The Promise: God will supply all your needs according to the riches of His glory in Christ Jesus.

The Plan: Do you believe God will supply all your needs today? Why? Why not?

Peace over Reputation

He gave up his place with God and made himself nothing. He was born as a man and became like a servant.

Philippians 2:7

When Christian authors like myself write devotionals using personal stories as part of a life application example, there is typically at least one topic that's just a little more personal than the others. Letting go of my reputation is mine.

Now that I have some distance from raising teen girls I can tell you why I personally struggled so much during that time. Yes, it was primarily scrambled hormones that caused a lot of chaos, as I mention throughout the book, but it was also my obsession about having a good reputation.

For a long time I truly believed that we were a solid Christian family, living out godly morals and values in good fashion, and we were. However, when the hormonal upheaval took place, and suddenly words, actions and attitudes were not as I thought they should be, I became overly concerned that our family reputation - a.k.a. *my* reputation - stays perfectly intact while we sorted things out. I eventually discovered that sometimes you need to choose peace over a perfect reputation.

The King James Version of Philippians 2: 7 says that Jesus *"made himself of no reputation."* In other words, when all was said and done, Jesus, who had a legitimate right to be concerned about His reputation as the Son of God, wasn't. He simply focused on doing the will of His father by serving others. Could you imagine how different it would have been if Jesus had focused all His attention on His reputation? Could you imagine how different things would be if we only focused on doing the will of the Father?

The Problem: I worry about my reputation.

The Promise: Jesus gave up His place with God and made Himself nothing.

The Plan: Are you overly worried about your reputation as a Christian mom?

Hope, *transitive verb*
 : To desire with expectation of obtainment
 : To expect with confidence

Different Perceptions

I pray also that you will have greater understanding in your heart.

Ephesians 1:18

I was invited to speak to a group of ladies for their annual mother/daughter breakfast. After much prayer I knew that God wanted me to share about a very personal time when my oldest daughter strayed and went in a completely different direction than expected. I was to share some of the heartache I felt along with the faithfulness God displayed during that time.

Pulling into the parking lot that morning, I sat in my car praying for the ladies I was about to speak to, when God posed an unexpected question to my heart: *If your daughter was here would you still share the same message?*

I thought it was a strange question, as my daughter rarely has opportunity to hear me speak. Nevertheless, I thought about the question and knew in my heart that even though it would be awkward I would share the same message.

Pushing the thought aside, I walked into the room where I was to speak, and while I was getting my things settled I felt a tap on my shoulder. I turned around and there was my daughter holding a beautiful bouquet of flowers for me. I was pleasantly surprised but also very concerned. How would she respond to what I had to share? Then I remembered the question God had whispered to my heart.

We snuck off to the powder room and I expressed my concerns to her. Her response was priceless. *"It's okay, Mom. You have your perception, and so do I."*

Her response assured me of three things: The irrational teen years were being replaced with maturity; scrambled hormones years bring different perspectives; and God is forever faithful.

The Problem: Our perspectives our different.

The Promise: I pray also that you will have greater understanding in your heart.

The Plan: What is your perspective of this season of your life?

Even Now Faith

But I know that even now God will give you anything you ask.

John 11:21-23

I love the story in the book of John that tells about the death of Lazarus. Lazarus and his sisters, Mary and Martha, were very close friends with Jesus. One day Lazarus became gravely ill. Concerned for their brother, the sisters sent word to Jesus to come quickly and heal their brother. Yet when the request was made to *come quickly*, Jesus took His time. By the time He finally reached the house of his dear friends, Lazarus had been dead and buried for four days. It should have been the end of the story, but it wasn't.

Seeing Jesus, Martha brings Him up to speed and says, "Lord, if You had been here, my brother would not have died. But I know that *even now* God will give You anything you ask." Martha had an "even now" faith, meaning that despite the way it looked, she was going to believe Jesus for the impossible. As we learn from the rest of the story, Jesus responded to her faith and raised Lazarus from the grave.

During the hormonal years, teens often make one poor decision after another, and because of their actions and choices, many moms begin to feel as if the beautiful dream they have for their child's life and future is dead and buried. What we learn from the story of Lazarus is that nothing but God has the final say. God knows the dreams moms have for their kids, and while things can get pretty wild during the teen years, when moms apply "even now" faith, God responds.

The Problem: The dreams I had have vanished.

The Promise: But I know that even now God will give you anything you ask.

The Plan: What dreams do you have for your kids, for yourself? It's time to use "even now" faith in God.

Follow Your Own Advice

I find rest in God; only he gives me hope.

Psalm 62:5

Feelings of hopelessness can come upon us for a variety of reasons. Being abandoned or forsaken by someone, feeling uninspired for far too long, sensing powerlessness to chart our own course in life or even spending too much time isolated from others can trigger bleak emotions. Off and on throughout the teen years when hormones collided, my daughters would experience feelings of bleakness. When this occurred I would try to encourage them to lean on God and place their hope in Him. But often, perhaps due to the typical teenage nature, they resisted the encouragement.

Continually being faced with their resistance to my advice, over time I gradually developed my own sense of hopelessness over the situation. I didn't realize that I had become so focused on them following what I was suggesting, to draw near to God for hope during feelings of bleakness, that I was no longer following my own advice.

Moms have a natural tendency to counsel and advise their children in every area of life so they will grow mentally, emotionally and spiritually strong. Unfortunately, in the midst of all the advice giving, we can easily forget the need to follow our own advice. Once I stopped trying to advise my daughters to place their hope in God during bleak times and instead concentrated on following my own advice first, change began to take place for all of us.

The Problem: I feel hopeless and don't know what to do.

The Promise: You, Lord, give true peace to those who depend on You, because they trust in You.

The Plan: If your daughter came to you with the very same problem you are struggling with, what advice would you give her? Do you follow your own advice? If not, ask God to give you the strength to do so.

It Takes a Village

Two people are better than one, because they get more done by working together.

Ecclesiastes 4:9

When my oldest daughter was in high school, she had a friend who was struggling with some very serious issues. One day she invited her friend to come to our house after explaining to her that I was someone she could talk to about her problems; that I was someone she could trust and who could offer help. This wasn't the first time my daughter told one of her hurting friends to talk to me about the problems they were dealing with, instead of them going off and doing something they would later regret. What an honor it was for me to know that my daughter genuinely felt that I had compassion and wisdom to offer her friends who were struggling with various issues.

Knowing she felt this way made it all the more difficult in her later teen years when she wasn't interested in the compassion and wisdom I had for *her*. I couldn't understand how my encouragement, counsel and guidance were good enough for her friends but not always good enough for her. Because of my fix-it nature, which is pretty much every mom's nature, it took me some time to figure it out.

The mother/daughter relationship is so emotionally intertwined that it's hard for a daughter to receive encouragement from her mom the same way she would from someone else. Sometimes daughters just need to reach out to someone else. Fortunately, there were a few godly mamas who encouraged my daughter during her trying times, just as I was able to encourage her friends during their time of need.

The Problem: Sometimes I can help other kids better than my own.

The Promise: Two people are better than one, because they get more done by working together.

The Plan: Remember that sometimes it takes a village to raise a child.

The One Real Guarantee

*He put his Spirit in our hearts to be a guarantee
for all he has promised.*

2 Corinthians 1:22

If you were to ask me for one bit of advice that would help curb the anxiety that many Christian moms struggle with in regards to the choices their children will make as they enter the teen years and on into young adulthood, I would have to say simply: *Accept the fact that there are no guarantees.*

Most mamas work hard at developing good behavior in their children, but as children maneuver their way through puberty and gradually become young adults, they often make irrational choices and do outlandish things, causing even the most God-trusting mama to suffer from much late-night anxiety.

The very best thing a mom can do is seek God daily for direction, guidance and the ability to be a consistently good example before her children. And even when we moms blow it, which we will do often, we can teach them the godly principle of confessing our shortcomings and accepting God's forgiveness as we continue our daily walk.

That is what we are suppose to do, the very best we can do. But even then there is no guarantee that our children will model our behavior or apply any of the godly principles we've taught them because just like us, our children were created for an individual relationship with God.

When a mom can remember to simply do her best and let God do the rest, she can release her anxieties to God's care. While we have no guarantees when it comes to the outcome of our children's choices and behavior, we do have a full guarantee in God.

The Problem: I want a guarantee.

The Promise: He put His Spirit in our hearts to be a guarantee for all He has promised.

The Plan: Do you want a guarantee? Read Ephesians 1:14.

Touch of Hope

*This hope will never disappoint us, because God
has poured out his love to fill our hearts.*

Romans 5:5

Every Sunday our pastor asks the congregation to turn around and greet a few people. I found myself uncomfortable with this ritual during an extended season of disappointment. The teen years were not going as smoothly as I had hoped. I was afraid that if I greeted too many church members, one just might notice the inner turmoil I was struggling with - the hopelessness I was feeling.

One Sunday, an elderly man I had never seen before walked toward my husband to greet him. He extended his hand, and I thought little of it until he did something completely unexpected. The unknown man reached out his arms and gently took my husband's face into his hands. He then stared deep into my husband's eyes and displayed the most genuine look I have ever seen.

Though the greeting was given to my husband, I felt it. It seemed as if this stranger looked right through my husband's eyes and right into my heart. Witnessing my typically guarded husband relax his face in the hands of this stranger struck me to my core and gave me hope.

The stranger didn't say any special words and certainly didn't know our situation, but in that moment I knew God had used the elderly man's gentle touch and genuine expression to let us know everything would be just fine.

The Problem: My situation is hopeless.

The Promise: This hope will never disappoint us, because God has poured out His love to fill our hearts.

The Plan: Studies have shown that setting small, achievable goals instills a sense of hope in an accomplishment. Take a moment to set a few small goals for yourself, beginning with reading scriptures about hope (e.g., Psalm 62:5, 1 Peter 1:21, Proverbs 24:14).

Confidence, noun
: The feeling of being certain that something will happen or that something is true

Building Confidence

I can do all things through Him who strengthens me.

Philippians 4:13

There are many defining moments throughout the teen years where lessons are learned and confidence is built. One of those lesson-learning moments came for both my oldest daughter and me one afternoon when I suggested we go bowling.

In her mind, I was already pushing it by wanting to be out in public with her. Nevertheless, she agreed and even seemed to be enjoying the company of her dorky mom - that is, until after I paid for our bowling game and the cashier told us which lane we were to play on.

Scanning the alley, my daughter quickly spotted a handful of her peers bowling on the lane right next to ours. She panicked and said, "Mom, I don't want to be here. I don't know how to bowl. Let's go."

I tried to be sensitive to her self-conscious teenage state of mind, but I wasn't about to waste money. We went round and round in a whispering battle of the wills.

"Let's go."

"We're staying."

"Mom, let's go."

"No, we are staying."

My daughter glared at me as if I was the worst mom ever. Was I? She was clearly uncomfortable. Should I be more understanding? My runaway thoughts were causing me to doubt. *Lord help me.*

"We are bowling!" I said.

Finally conceding, my daughter grabbed her bowling ball, walked at a snail's pace to the bowling line then released the ball down the lane. Hanging her head, she turned and walked away without seeing the results. She had bowled a strike in front of her peers. She was encouraged, and so was I.

The Problem: Sometimes as a mom I lack confidence too.

The Promise: *I can do all things through Him who strengthens me* (Philippians 4:13).

The Plan: Build your confidence today, Mom, by spending the day thinking positive thoughts on purpose.

Run the Race

Let us run the race that is before us and never give up.

Hebrews 12:1

This book that you hold in your hand is a direct result of applying Hebrews 12:1 to my life.

Fourteen years ago I felt a nudging from the Holy Spirit to write with the purpose of inspiring readers in their everyday walk with God. It was a very exciting time as I was able to share stories of how God was working in my own life with my family.

My children were at the perfect age for me to write faith-based stories. I had plenty of material to pull from as they were happily involved with school, church and friends. God-stuff just naturally seemed to ooze out of them. Because they were at an innocent age it was easy for me to write endlessly about the goodness, faithfulness and love of God.

Then my oldest girl entered high school and began dealing with bigger teen issues, followed by her younger sister a few years later, who had teen issues of her own. Throw in my early menopause, a demanding job, marriage and overall life, and I no longer felt quite as inspired to write warm, fuzzy faith articles as I once had. After a while I considered the idea of giving up on this ministry of writing. Every time I wanted to quit God would remind of Hebrews 12:1. Run the race, don't give up. The verse not only encouraged me to keep writing but reminded me that I needed to keep running the race with raising my teenagers. If I didn't give up, I'd see the reward.

The Problem: Sometimes I want to give up.

The Promise: Let us run the race that is before us and never give up.

The Plan: Whether it's raising kids, ministry, marriage or life, recommit to run the race God has set before you and never give up.

Stare Down the Enemy with Confidence

*They are confident and will not be afraid; they
will look down on their enemies.*

Psalm 112:8

Confidence is an interesting thing. When you have it, you feel sure of yourself and your actions regardless of what anyone else may think. But when your confidence falters, everything you were so sure of is questionable.

As moms, there are days when we are confident and sure in dealing with our teenagers, and there are days our confidence is nowhere to be found.

I experienced a severe lack of confidence during a period of time when one of my daughters was consistently challenging me. It seemed like whatever I was saying or doing with her just wasn't working. I shared my frustration with a friend who wisely reminded me of how the enemy loves to stir up friction, and that I didn't need to be discouraged or afraid that my parenting skills were failing. I simply needed to look beyond my teenager and address the enemy.

I knew from Scripture that my friend had a good point. My lack of confidence was because I was focusing on the wrong thing. The next time my daughter challenged me, instead of looking at her as if she was the enemy and getting into yet another heated hormone battle, I confronted the real enemy directly by quoting Mathew 16:23, *"Get behind me Satan."*

I will never forget the look of surprise in my daughter's eyes. In that moment, I believe we both understood that enough was enough. Instead of fighting each other, it was time to stare down the enemy with confidence and tell him to hit the bricks.

The Problem: Sometime I lack confidence.

The Promise: They are confident and will not be afraid; they will look down on their enemies.

The Plan: In what areas do you need to stare down the enemy with confidence?

Statement of Purpose

Let us hold firmly to the hope that we have confessed, because we can trust God to do what he promised.

Hebrews 10:23

In April of 2002 we moved from our adorable starter home to a more spacious, family-friendly home just a few short blocks away. A few weeks before the move my husband and I sat on our living room floor with our three kids and thought it would be nice to find a specific scripture that would represent our family in our new home.

I found the idea incredibly meaningful. I just knew that whatever scripture we agreed upon would become our family statement of purpose for our new home and forever.

We tossed around a few favorite scriptures until someone suggested 2 Corinthian 6:16-17 (NIV). *"We are the temple of the living God. As God has said: "I will live with them and walk among them, and I will be their God, and they will be my people. Therefore, Come out from them and be separate, says the Lord."*

That was the one. We all agreed this verse was God's promise and fully represented our hearts. He was our God, and we were His people. I typed up the scripture on gold-rimmed paper with the words *Our Statement of Purpose* written across the top, framed it and hung it in our new home.

A few years later when scrambled hormones took effect, I began to question if our statement of purpose still applied, but through Hebrews 10:23 God reminded me that we can trust Him to do what He promised. He is still our God, and we are still His people.

The Problem: I've lost sight of my purpose.

The Promise: Let us hold firmly to the hope that we have confessed, because we can trust God to do what He promised.

The Plan: Do you have a personal Statement of Purpose?

Sweat It Out

I know your soul is doing fine, and I pray that
you are doing well in every way.

3 John 1:2

D o you love going to the gym? Do you love jumping on the cardio machines and running until you are drenched in sweat? How about free weights? Do you love grabbing the dumbbells and doing countless reps until you're muscles are spent? I do.

Okay, okay that's not true. The truth is, I am a member of a gym. It's very clean, has great equipment and it's close to my house. I like going there and showing the girls at the front desk my member's badge so I can get special points added to my account, though I'm still not sure what the points are for. I don't even mind power walking on a treadmill or using ten-pound weights to do a few reps, but if you want to know the truth, I hate to sweat.

If there was a way to exercise while sitting on my couch and without sweating one bit I would be one happy camper. Nevertheless, I go to the gym and do what I need to do despite the yucky sweating for one main reason: It strengthens me physically, emotionally and spiritually.

When hormones go crazy, whether they be your teen daughter's or your own, exercising releases the tension, brings clarity and calms the emotions. How do I know? I spent many days at the gym during the scrambled hormone years working out my frustration, listening to worship music and talking with God. It was during those "worship workouts" that I moved beyond the sweat and saw a change.

The Problem: Sometimes I'm too tense.

The Promise: I know your soul is doing fine, and I pray that you are doing well in every way.

The Plan: Listen to your favorite worship music while exercising a few times a week. You'll see a change.

Their Purpose, Your Purpose

People may make plans in their minds, but the
Lord decides what they will do.

Proverbs 16:9

I'm sitting here trying to think of one mom, just one mom who I personally know (and I know many) that hasn't lost sight of her purpose at some point throughout parenting. As moms we are all but obsessed with helping our kids find their way, their purpose in life. From the moment our babies do anything that we might consider spectacular (which is just about everything) we begin thinking that the spectacular thing they do is indeed their life purpose.

When my oldest daughter was five years old she was so sensitive to the needs of others that she would just give, give and give. When my youngest daughter was four, she was strong willed, determined and spoke her mind, especially about the things of God.

As I considered my girls' opposing personalities, I was convinced that my oldest was destined be a missionary and my youngest a preacher. As far as I was concerned their purpose for life was set, and I viewed everything from that particular perspective. Now that's not to say that it would never happen, but I became so focused on what I considered to be their purpose that I forgot about my own.

The most important purpose for a mom is to raise her babies, preschoolers, and yes, even her teenagers in the ways of the Lord. We have been given the privilege to equip our children to seek God for themselves so that they can discover their purpose in this life in order to fulfill the will of God, not the will of mom.

The Problem: Sometimes I assume I know what's best.

The Promise: People may make plans in their minds, but the Lord decides what they will do.

The Plan: To keep things in proper perspective ask: What is my purpose as a mom?

Assurance, *noun*
   : The state of being sure or certain about something

After All I've Done

*He will not forget the work you did and the love
you showed for him by helping his people.*

Hebrews 6:10

There comes a time in the life for almost every mom who is raising a teenager girl when she feels compelled to shout at the top of her lungs to anyone who will listen the golden phrase, *After all I have done for you, this is how you treat me!*

The "After all I've done" pity-party feelings started brewing just beneath my own emotional surface during my oldest daughter's teen years, but bubbled up and over the top the year she didn't acknowledge me on Mother's Day. That was the first time I realized what emotional power a teenage daughter has over her mom.

Moms give all they have to their children from the moment they are born. That's why when hormonal changes take place during the teen years and the natural stages of pulling away and sometimes being insensitive begin, moms rarely handle it with grace.

When my teenager forgot me on Mother's Day, I wanted to teach her a lesson and not be quite so caring all the time. Instead I brought my bruised feelings to God. He quickly reminded me that I'm serving Him when I love and care for my children, and to hold back that love and care over hurt feelings would not bring Him honor.

Now, many years later, my daughter always finds ways to make me feel like a very special mama, and neither of us forget or hold back any love.

The Problem: I get tired of giving.

The Promise: He will not forget the work you did and the love you showed for Him by helping His people.

The Plan: Ask God for the strength to keep serving Him by loving and caring for the children He has given you, even "after all you've done."

Change Is Coming

*Look at the new thing I am going to do. It is
already happening. Don't you see it? I will make
a road in the desert and rivers in the dry land.*

Isaiah 43:19

This morning I received the good news that my younger daughter and her boyfriend are officially engaged. The timing of this news couldn't be more perfect. Here I am, coming to the end of writing this devotional book geared toward encouraging moms with hormonal teenage daughters, who may wonder if they'll ever make it through this rocky stage, and I get a call from my own daughter reminding me of God's faithfulness.

I remember asking God when both girls were little to allow their teen years to go smoothly, to help them ease into the transition from flowers and dolls to makeup and boys effortlessly. It seemed like a reasonable request until puberty hit and all the physical and emotional changes that naturally take place with a teenager showed up.

God did not grant my request for smooth and effortless teen years. It was pretty bumpy all the way. However, through all the ups and downs, God taught me how to pray for my daughters, and for myself. He also taught me how to believe beyond what was taking place and to trust Him for the long haul.

Whenever there were a number of teen-issue days in a row I would find myself wondering if things would ever change. Instead of asking God to make it smoother, I learned to accept how things were and believe that He was working behind the scenes to bring about the needed change.

The Problem: Will it ever change?

The Promise: "Look at the new thing I am going to do. It is already happening. Don't you see it?"

The Plan: Fill in the blank: God is doing a new thing in _____

God Cares When You Care

Indeed, the very hairs of your head are all numbered."

Luke 12:7

In our old home we had a pool fountain called a sheer descent that I absolutely loved. Whenever I would flick on the fountain switch and listen to the soothing sounds of the water I would feel a sense of calm come over me.

Even my prayer times and Bible reading seemed more meaningful when done with the bubbling sounds of the water in the background. Many hours were spent there, praying for my girls, asking God to be with them, particularly during the turbulent teen years.

When we downsized from our home a number of years later, I didn't mind having a smaller house, but I sure did miss the peaceful sounds of the sheer descent.

That first spring in our new place I walked into the nursery of a local store and immediately heard the familiar sound of bubbling water. Rushing to see where it came from, I discovered a perfect handcrafted fountain that was completely beyond my budget. I sighed and thought, *Maybe one day.*

Three years passed, and from time to time I would remind God of my desire for a fountain, wondering if it was a silly desire. Recently, to my surprise, the fountain went on sale...for only ten percent of its original price. I couldn't believe it! It was within my budget.

When I set up the fountain and heard the peaceful water sounds again, I thought about how much God cares. No desire is too silly to Him. After all, He knows the number of hairs on our heads, so why wouldn't He care about the things that we care about?

The Problem: Does anyone care?

The Promise: Indeed, the very hairs of your head are all numbered.

The Plan: Consider what you care about most Mom, big or small, and then read Luke 12:7 again.

God Isn't Slow

*The Lord is not slow in doing what he promised
- the way some people understand slowness. But
God is being patient with you.*

2 Peter 3:9

It was my oldest daughter's fifteenth birthday, and we had planned a small party that would include Mom, Dad, brother, sister, and most importantly, girlfriends from high school. These friends were the ones my daughter really wanted at her party, the ones that for whatever reason made her feel extra special. Having them there meant that she would have the best party ever.

Unfortunately, as the party day arrived, most of the girls who were invited called to cancel or didn't bother to call at all. Having your birthday party crumble is devastating for a teenage girl, particularly when so-called friends flake. I quickly scrambled to put another plan together, and while we managed to have a party after all with a few loyal family friends, knowing her original plans failed was a sting to my daughter's sensitive heart.

Though I had no control over the flaky friends, I felt terrible because, like most teen girls, I knew my daughter struggled with feelings of rejection. I had often prayed and asked God to help her in this very area. I trusted that He heard my prayers, but on that day I wondered why it was taking Him so long to answer.

Like with so many things that happen, I later realized how God used that time of disappointment to build stronger character in my daughter and in me. God wasn't slow after all. He was just working behind the scene.

The Problem: Sometimes God is slow.

The Promise: The Lord is not slow in doing what He promised - the way some people understand slowness. But God is being patient with you.

The Plan: Plant a flower seed in soil. Keep a daily journal on what it's like waiting for your flower to bloom.

I Believe, I Doubt

I do believe! Help me believe more!

Mark 9:24

I love the story found in Mark 9 where a father brings his son to Jesus for healing. The father explains how his son is consumed at times by an evil spirit and that when the spirit takes over it throws his son to the ground, causing him to foam at the mouth and act out in frightening ways.

The father pleads with Jesus saying, "If you can do anything for him, please have pity on us and help us." Jesus replies, "You said, 'If you can!' All things are possible for the one who believes."

The father quickly cries out a profound response, "I do believe! Help me believe more!"

Like the father in the story, Christian moms believe. They believe it's their God-given privilege to raise their children in the ways of the Lord, and so they do. However, there are times when things just don't go as planned, especially during the teen years when emotions and attitude are at a high. String too many of the intense teen moments together, and even then strongest

91

Christian mom can struggle with her faith and belief. That's when stories like the one found in Mark 9 offer great insight on what a believing mom needs to do.

The circumstances may be different, but a believing mom needs to have enough faith to bring her teen to Jesus and enough honesty to say, *I believe You are a healer and can do all things, but I also get overwhelmed and doubt. I need Your help, Jesus, to believe even more than I say I do.*

The Problem: Sometimes I doubt.

The Promise: I do believe! Help me believe more!

The Plan: Acronyms are great ways to remember truths. Consider this acronym, for example:

Basic
Instruction
Before
Leaving
Earth

Create your own an acronym for **BELIEVE**.

The Sun and I

*You made the moon to mark the seasons, and
the sun always knows when to set.*

Psalm 104:19

When I first read the first half of Psalm 104:19, *"You made the moon to mark the seasons,"* I thought it was nice of God to use the moon as a calendar for us. But when I read the second half, *"The sun always knows when to set,"* I was a wee envious.

The sun, a huge glowing sphere of hot gas, which according to astronomers could fit 1.3 million earths inside of it, knows exactly when to set each and every day. No struggle, no confusion; just rising and setting where it was created to without a hitch.

Then there's me: a 5' 4", 140-pound mama who can't even figure out what I'm doing from one day to the next without getting a brain cramp. *If only I was more like the sun.* Of course, comparing my role to the sun is silly, but so is one mom's tendency to compare herself to another mom.

We don't compare too much when all is well, but let trouble strike and suddenly a mom finds herself envious of that "other mom." The mom who seems to have it together, the one who keeps cool under pressure, never has hormonal break downs, and just seems to know exactly how to be perfectly set, just like the sun.

Here's the thing: the sun only knows where to set because it relies on God. All moms, supposedly perfect or not, must do the same. There's no need to compare yourself to another; simply rely on God for you to be the mom He created you to be.

The Problem: Other moms have it all together.

The Promise: *You made the moon to mark the seasons, and the sun always knows when to set.*

The Plan: Give a compliment to another mom, and then give yourself two.

Fearless, *adjective*
  : Free from fear

Forget About It

Forget what happened before, and do not think about the past. Look at the new thing I am going to do. It is already happening. Don't you see it?

Isaiah 43:18-19

I have often heard that things get harder right before a breakthrough. I found that to be true as my youngest daughter came to the end of her teen years. We had been through so many ups and down that I was growing weary in seeking God for change on her behalf.

After a while, all I could see were the problems, the challenges, the teen issues we had been dealing with for so long. Scriptures like Isaiah 43:19 - *"Look at the new thing I am going to do. It is already happening. Don't you see it?"* - seemed like wishful thinking.

Then one evening my daughter made a small gesture that sparked a flicker of hope.

I had placed a little blanket across my lap while watching television. My daughter was sitting nearby and, as it had been for some time, the words between us were few. While adjusting myself in the chair, the blanket fell to the floor. Without a word, she leaned over and gently draped the blanket across my lap before turning back toward the television. I was in shock.

It wasn't her nature to show acts of tenderness in general, but throughout the ever-changing hormonal teen years, any signs of affection had gone completely out the window. She had no idea how that small gesture helped me look past the problems we had and toward the new thing God was doing.

The Problem: I only see problems.

The Promise: Forget what happened before. Look at the new thing I am going to do.

The Plan: Write the pros and cons about your teenager on a piece of paper. Then completely shred the "con" side of the list and just focus on the pros.

He Hears Our Cries

The Lord has heard my cry for help; the Lord will answer my prayer.

Psalm 6:9

In the early stage of the teen years, when hormonal breakdowns occurred only here and there, both daughters were quick to confide in me. Through teary eyes they would share how life was so unfair because their so-called friends were not as nice as they had thought, or that the boys they considered cute started acting ridiculous, and so on.

Whatever the issue was on those emotional days, the conversation would always include my daughters feeling so incredibly hurt and wanting to know just how long the hurt would last.

At a time when life seemed so unreasonable for my teenage girls and their only thought was how long until the hurt goes away, the best I could do was reassure them that everything would be okay.

Fast forward a few weeks, months, maybe a year into teen life when hormonal breakdowns became the norm, and instead of confiding in Mama during this stage, both began acting as if Mama was the enemy.

I remember hitting that exact same stage with my mom when I was a teen. Nevertheless, it didn't make it easier when I experienced it with my own daughters. During this stage I was the one crying out, "This is unfair! When will the hurt go away?" The one I needed reassurance from was God, and when I called out, He answered.

The Problem: How long will I hurt?

The Promise: The Lord has heard my cry for help; the Lord will answer my prayer.

The Plan: Read Psalm 6. Written by King David during a time when he sought forgiveness and restoration, his honesty with God about his hurt and his discovery of how God heard his cry and answered is a wonderful reminder of how we as moms can be honest with God and know that He hears our cry.

Heavenly Questions

Now I know only a part, but then I will know
fully, as God has known me.

1 Corinthians 13:12

When I get to heaven and stand face to face with my Creator, the first thing I am going to do is ask if we can sit and talk for a while. And I mean a long, long, long while. As the Word says, this side of heaven we "only know in part," so I will have a pretty lengthy list of heavenly questions.

Naturally I will ask the intense type of questions that I assume most believers would want more detailed answers to, like why so much suffering for innocent people, and why things like racism and human trafficking were ever allowed. Once we discuss the reasons behind those serious concerns my next very important question that I personally want answers to will be, "What was up with all the hormones, God?"

Seriously, I want to know why God created pre-menopausal moms and raging hormone teenage daughters to live under the same roof, to love each other so intensely yet manage to push each other to the edge due to all the scrambled hormones.

I am sure God will have a wonderful explanation for it all, and I really do look forward to hearing all about the methods He chose. But the best I can tell from this side of heaven is that God created us somewhat like beautiful stones, and we have rough edges that need smoothing out to show our full beauty. I believe the complex and often hormonal mother/daughter relationship is just one of the many "sandpapers" God uses to smooth out each other's rough edges. I can't wait to ask Him all about it.

The Problem: There are many things I do not understand.

The Promise: Now I know only a part, but then I will know full.

The Plan: Make a list of heavenly questions for God.

In God's Hand

I am the Lord your God, who holds your right hand, and I tell you, Don't be afraid. I will help you.

Isaiah 41:13

I had my first taste of what parenting the teen years might be like when my younger daughter was only three years old. We were taking a walk together and were about to cross the street. Before stepping off the curb, I took my daughter's small hand into mine and looked both ways. Seeing no cars I said to my daughter, "Okay, sweetie, let's go."

The first few steps were a perfect mother and daughter moment as my little girl rested her trusting hand in mine allowing me to lead her safely across the street. But something strange happened mid-way. I don't know what caused it, perhaps a hormone from the future found its way into her toddler brain, but a mood shift took place.

My little angel went from willingly placing her hand in mind to pulling it away sharply, letting me know she wanted to cross the street without my help. I scrambled to maintain the grip on her hand and said, "You need to hold Mommy's hand to be safe, sweetie."

But she just wasn't hearing it. She fought me the rest of the way across the street, unable to understand that Mama was trying to help her.

A dozen years later as a teenager she fought me all the way on many things. While I was still inclined to hold her hand and keep her safe, God showed me that His hand is bigger than mine.

The Problem: I need to release my grip.

The Promise: I am the Lord your God, who holds your right hand.

The Plan: Trace your right hand on a piece of paper. Write Isaiah 41:13 across the top. Now fill the hand with what concerns you. Remember God's hand is bigger than yours. He won't let go.

Peanut Butter Pastor

The Lord will always lead you.

Isaiah 58:11

When my girls were little and I was their primary teacher of all God-things, they thought I was the coolest. I'm sure when they read this devotion they will roll their eyes and quickly deny that they ever thought Mom was the coolest. But it's true, I tell you. For a short time I was cool in their eyes, and I bet you were too.

I started catching little clues that I might not be the "coolest" anymore when my girls hit the double-digit years and no longer showed interest in our favorite pastime of cuddling on the couch or sitting close at the dining room table to talk about God. Oh, they still believed, but my God-talk was becoming a bore.

I knew my "coolest Mommy" status was done the night my daughter came home from her youth group and excitedly told me every detail about the most amazing pastor in the whole wide universe. Playing a Bible teaching game, the youth pastor said that if he lost the wager he would put globs of peanut butter under his armpits. What teen wouldn't love to see that?

Sure enough, after losing the wager, the youth pastor stayed true to his word and spread sticky peanut butter all over his armpits - all for the sake of sharing the gospel with teenagers. *Oh Lordy, how could I ever compete with that?*

That night I came to grips with two things: One, Mr. Peanut Butter Pits was the new "coolest." Two, though my role as the primary spiritual influence for my girls was changing, God would always find ways to teach them, even if it was through an armpit full of peanut butter.

The Problem: I still want to be the leader.

The Promise: The Lord will always lead you.

The Plan: Is your role changing? If so, will you trust God to lead your children?

You Can Handle the Truth

You will know the truth, and the truth will make you free.

John 8:32

I've been walking with God long enough to know that when problems arise there is really no better alternative than to seek help from God through prayer. I found this especially true whenever I freaked out over teenage issues that seemed to come up all too often. I'm sure all you moms of teens know what I mean.

My tendency toward freaking out over teen issues hit an all-time high when I was experiencing full-blown pre-menopausal symptoms. On one such occasion I found myself coming unglued again over an issue with one of my daughters. Fortunately, I had just connected with an encouraging group of prayer warrior ladies, who were committed to praying on behalf of me and my daughter. One wise woman from the group gave me a copy of a prayer on breaking strongholds.

Filling in the blanks with my daughter's name I read this portion of the prayer night and day:

I loose every fear that _____

will be disappointed and hurt further if her unmet needs are revealed. I loose every wrong belief that she has ever had that You wouldn't "fix" every single hurt and unresolved issue in her life, making her whole and strong - filled with Your joy and peace.

The more I read this prayer on behalf of my daughter, the more I understood that I needed this prayer too. God's Word is truth, and yes, His truth can bring freedom for our children. But, we must not forget to allow His Word to set us free as well.

The Problem: I need to be reminded of the truth.

The Promise: *The truth will make you free.*

The Plan: Add your name to the blank above, and let God speak to your heart.

Release, *verb*
: To stop holding (someone or something)

Let God Do the Fixing

The Lord watches over those who follow him.

Psalm 97:10

My youngest daughter played soccer for three years through the Parks and Recreation department. After making the All-Star team her third season, she decided to take the next step and try out for a Hi-Comp team. During tryouts she ran various drills with confidence and competed in the one-on-one scrimmages with ease, earning her a spot on a Division 3 traveling team.

She was twelve years old and having the time of her life. She made new friends on the team and developed her playing skills rapidly. She was thirteen when tryouts rolled around again, and that cloud of insecurity that tends to follow teen girls had officially landed.

On the day of the tryouts she suddenly refused to go. She knew not trying out meant she couldn't play for that team for a year, but she was too intimidated to try. During the days that followed I noticed how downhearted she was, and so I found another coach from a different team who was holding tryouts the following weekend.

The team was a U-15 team, two years older than my daughter, but I as explained the situation the coach kindly agreed to let her participate in tryouts simply to help her face her insecurities. On the day of tryouts my daughter was so upset that I was making her face her insecurities that she took her anger out on the field. She made the team.

While my desire to fix things seemed to help in that situation, "fixing" became an unhealthy pattern of mine. We Christian moms tell our kids that God is their provider, yet we often step in, fix their problems and eliminate consequences, resulting in our kids never really needing to rely on God to provide for their needs - whether it's soccer-related or something much bigger.

The Problem: I try to fix everything.

The Promise: The Lord watches over those who follow Him.

The Plan: Put down your handy-mom tools and trust God do the fixing.

Don't Take It Personally

The wise are patient; they will be honored if they ignore insults.

Proverbs 19:11

When my girls were in elementary school and came home crushed over hurtful words unexpectedly spoken by a classmate, I often advised them to just ignore what was said. I tried to explain that many times people who say hurtful things have their own problems and don't think about how their words affect others. I tried to encourage my girls not to take the hurtful words so personally.

It sounded like great advice until my girls became teenagers and began saying things like: "You don't understand me. You don't care. You're too strict, you're too this and you're too that." Like most moms, I knew exactly how much I cared for my kids and how much I did for them, so when those types of comments came spewing out of my teenagers, it never dawned on me that they might have their own things going on. Instead I took their insensitive words personally and felt insulted. Later I learned from my girls that there were times when I had other things going on as well, and I unintentionally said insensitive things to them, leaving them feeling insulted too.

Proverbs 19:11 is truly wise advice, but let's face it; sometimes ignoring an insult is difficult, especially between mother and daughter. Yet God says we will be honored if we don't take it all so personally.

The Problem: I feel insulted.

The Promise: The wise are patient; they will be honored if they ignore insults.

The Plan: Next time you feel you're being insulted try not to take it so personally. Refocus your attention from what was said to how it made you feel. When the time is right, communicate those feelings in love. After all, maybe it's not about you but what the other person is going through.

Leave the Putty Alone

*Let your patience show itself perfectly in what
you do.*

James 1:4

When my younger daughter was nine years old we
went to the orthodontist to get impressions
made of her teeth so she could get braces. We
sat in the waiting room together, and when her name was
called I naturally followed right behind her, just in case
she needed me.

Taking a small tray created to fit over the teeth, the
dental assistant filled it with something called alginate, a
powder mixed with water to the consistency of gooey
putty. She then put the putty into the tray and placed the
tray in my daughter's mouth.

While the dental assistant pressed firmly on the tray,
a look of panic shot across my daughter's face. I knew in
my head that the hardening of the putty was necessary for
a good impression, yet my Mama emotions told me that
my baby was uncomfortable, and I needed to do
something.

It was probably only fifteen seconds, but it seemed like hours as I watched my daughter's eyes grow saucer size over the putty in her mouth. I couldn't take it anymore. I smacked the sweet dental assistant's hand out of the way instinctively then quickly grabbed the handle of the tray and pulled it from my daughter's mouth. Realizing what I had done after the fact, I apologized then offered to wait in the lobby as they redid the procedure.

Stepping in too soon to rescue my daughters from being uncomfortable was a pattern that continued throughout their teen years and that I occasionally still struggle with. But I am learning that swooping in and picking them up too soon often gets in the way of what God is trying to teach them.

The Problem: Sometimes I get in the way.

The Promise: Let your patience show itself perfectly in what you do.

The Plan: You're not always called to be the rescuer.

Let Go of the Fear

I will not be afraid, because the Lord is my helper.

Hebrews 13:6

Early in my Christian walk God showed me that I needed to let go of the reigns and let Him lead. This wasn't an easy task, as I was used to doing things my way for many years. As I started to let go, I struggled greatly with fear. This struggle would have been hard regardless, but because I had two small girls for whom I wanted to be a good example, it bothered me even more. I longed to be a perfect Christian mom, but in truth I was still learning how to just be me in Christ.

I worked through a great deal of my fear issues during my girls' younger years and grew greatly in my relationship with God. As they came into their teen years, however, I noticed old fears returning and wasn't sure why.

Kids are a mom's kryptonite. The love we have for them is over the moon, which is why we hold onto the reigns so tightly. When the teen years arrive, there's the fear that every good thing that we have tried to instill into their lives thus far will be tossed aside, and utter chaos will take over. With all the rewiring that has taken place in their brains since puberty, a measure of chaos usually does pay a visit, and as in my case, old and new fears can be triggered. While it can be a scary time, it can also be a good time - a time when God can remind moms (and their teens) that He is their helper and there's no need to fear.

The Problem: I hold on tightly because I'm afraid.

The Promise: I will not be afraid, because the Lord is my helper.

The Plan: Ask God to help you learn how to let go of your fear grip.

Soul Food Sunday

May the Lord give you all that you ask for.

Psalm 20:5

In 1997 I went to see the widely acclaimed movie *Soul Food*, which tells the story of a growing family's traditional weekly dinner gathering as a way to stay connected. I loved the movie so much that I was inspired to create the same tradition with my husband and children. Soul Food Sunday was to be our special time together with extra special homemade food that somehow made everything just perfect. I believed holding to that Sunday dinner would keep us on track and help us all stay close in faith and as a family, particularly as the kids got older.

At the time when Soul Food Sunday dinner became my priority, my girls were only ten and four. As Mama, I still held complete control over the dinner flow, so creating Soul Food Sunday was a piece of cake.

However, as the family grew and my girls became teens with their own thoughts and ideas of what was meaningful for them, having a standing commitment to meet at the table for a special "let's connect" weekly family dinner was not on their priority list.

By the time my oldest was eighteen and ready to move out to participate in a yearlong ministry program, I had all but badgered her with my idea of needing to maintain Soul Food Sunday once she moved out. Over time God showed me that my desire for keeping the family close was good, but my insistence on having it done a particular way wasn't giving Him much room to move. When I let go of my plan of how to stay connected, God showed me His.

The Problem: I have my plans.

The Promise: May the Lord give you all that you ask for.

The Plan: What is your plan for keeping the family connected? Now ask God for His.

Don't Be a Fool

Foolish people lose their tempers, but wise people control theirs.

Proverbs 29:11

O ne of my co-workers who had just came back from maternity leave after having her first daughter, asked me a question. "Monica, do you ever get mad?"

Apparently, during the time we had worked together prior to her going on maternity leave and again upon her return, she was under the impression that I never got angry. "You're always so happy and positive," she added.

It was a wonderful compliment, but the moment she asked the question, my mind flashed back to a time when one of my teenage daughters gave me that well-known disrespectful teenage eye roll at the wrong time, and I completely lost it.

Truthfully, I lost it a number of times throughout the teen years. On this particular occasion, my daughter had set her purse on the kitchen counter when our conversation began to heat up. I was trying to once again calmly explain the household rules to her when she responded with a full-blown eye roll. That's all it took; I'd had enough. I shoved her purse to the floor in anger and went on a ranting spree for who knows how long.

My ranting sprees had become more frequent the deeper we got into teen years and would have probably continued if God hadn't brought Proverbs 29:11 to my attention. Feeling angry regarding my daughter's disrespect wasn't the issue; giving full vent to my anger and acting a fool was.

"Oh yes, I get mad," I confessed to my sweet co-worker while silently thanking God for showing me the importance of submitting my anger to Him instead of being a fool.

The Problem: Sometimes I lose my temper.

The Promise: Foolish people lose their tempers, but wise people control theirs.

The Plan: Write out Proverbs 29:11 with a permanent marker on the outside bottom of a mug you regularly drink from. Be sure to turn it over and sneak a peek often.

Content, *adjective*
    : Pleased and satisfied
    : Not needing more

You'll Always Be the Seed

This is what the story means: The seed is God's message.

Luke 8:11

When my youngest daughter was ten years old she spent one evening searching a box of cards that had scriptures on one side and words of encouragement on the other. Finding the one she liked, she pulled out a pen and paper and copied the words. Later she came to me and said in a sweet, gentle voice, "Mommy, I picked this for you."

The note read "You are the seed that decides the harvest around you." The she added her own P.S. to the note, which said, "He loves you."

I cried my eyes out when I read her note because the words she shared were true. As Mom I was the seed that decided the harvest around me. As I allowed God to pour into my life, I was able to pour into my children and see a harvest.

The memory of that special evening crossed my mind many times during the teen years, especially during arguments when both of our voices went from sweet and gentle to loud and aggravated. *How things sure have changed*, I often thought during those emotionally driven tiffs. But had they really?

Sure, some aspects had changed. Instead of spending evenings digging through scripture boxes, my daughter was now focused on meeting the demands of high school. Instead of primarily being a stay-at-home mom, I now focused on working more hours. However, regardless of the phase of life we were in, as Mom, I was still the seed that decided the harvest around me, and so are you.

The harvest isn't always obvious during the teen years, but God assures us that we will have a harvest from the seeds we plant.

The Problem: Things have changed.

The Promise: The seed is God's message.

The Plan: What harvest do you want? What seeds are you planting?

Write It Out

Be Still and Know that I am God.

Psalm 46:10

I have never been one for tattoos. Mostly likely because in my younger years I was told that writing on your skin with an ink pen was taboo, and if washable ink was taboo then how much worse would it be to have permanent ink put into your skin through a needle?

While I still tend to be of that mindset, I did gain a better understanding as to why one is compelled to blanket their skin with permanent ink after both of my daughters decided to get tattoos that represented their deepest convictions. My oldest daughter went first with an imprint of her son's newborn feet tattooed on her back. I could understand that sentiment as my grandson has the cutest feet ever. Then my younger daughter went for a tattoo that spoke of broken wings learning to fly. I could certainly understand that sentiment as well.

While I don't believe I could ever bring myself to go the permanent "taboo" ink route, throughout the scrambled hormone years, I too felt inclined to express my deepest convictions and did so with my own little ink.

During one of the many "I've reached my max" moments, I took a black writing pen and wrote on the underside of my wrist, beneath a bracelet, where no one could see but me and God: "Be still and know…"

I kept it there for a few weeks, re-writing it whenever it began to fade. It was the reminder I needed to stop reacting to circumstances and instead remain still and trust God as a woman, a wife and a mom.

The Problem: I need reminders.

The Promise: Be still and know that I am God.

The Plan: Write out various scriptures, such as Psalm 46:10 on note cards to help you remember that you can trust God.

Have Some Good Medicine

A happy heart is like good medicine.

Proverbs 17:22

A ll moms know that beautiful feeling of unconditional love when they hear their toddler say, "My mommy is the best mommy in the whole wide world," and mean it.

When you experience that kind of love from your baby girl it's hard to imagine that your relationship would go any other way. But then the crazy, irrational teen years set in and before long, any sign of unconditional love for Mom seems to go into hiding. You're no longer the best mommy in the world; instead you're that annoying lady who lives in the same house, who is bossy and knows absolutely nothing.

Having two daughters five and a half years apart meant that I had the treat of dealing with hormone madness back to back. Just as the fog lifted from my oldest girl, it magically found its way to my younger one.

While I consider myself a pretty chipper person, during that time my chipper-ness was often in hiding.

The more teen girl drama came up, the more serious minded I became.

One day after yet another eye-rolling teen moment, I looked in the mirror and noticed a deep crease developing between my brows. It was the exact same crease I noticed as a teenager that my mom had, and now I knew why.

Having to discipline, correct and battle with your teenager regularly can leave some pretty deep facial creases. Sometimes being a good, responsible mom causes you to forget the importance of nurturing your soul and laughing in the midst of being responsible.

The Problem: I'm serious all the time.

The Promise: A happy heart is like good medicine.

The Plan: To begin nurturing your soul with laughter, enjoy this quote found all over the Internet these days. *"I smile because you are my daughter. I laugh because there is nothing you can do about it."*

Fill Me with Joy

Being with you will fill me with joy.

Acts 2:28

Most people are familiar with and find humor in the saying, *"If Mama ain't happy, ain't nobody happy."* I have to admit that every time I hear it I have a deep desire to jump up and down and high-five somebody while shouting "Amen!"

Experiencing pre-menopausal symptoms years before I would have expected to caused me to teeter on an emotional fine line, particularly when it came to dealing with my teenagers. My overactive hormones caused me to be easily irritated with them because their overactive hormones were causing them to be easily irritated with me. It was a vicious cycle, I tell you. One that I thought would only be resolved if everyone just understood, *"If Mama ain't happy..."* You get my point.

The more I wanted to use that saying as my go-to reason for my lack of joy during hormone flurries, the more God revealed that my joy wasn't based on pre-menopause or no menopause, perfectly behaved teens or no teens. Maintaining my joy had to do with spending time with Him and allowing the fruit of His Spirit, including His joy, to fill me.

I read an article by Joyce Meyer, "Seven Secrets to Keeping Your Joy," in *Charisma* magazine, which shared a few simple secrets to having joy. I believe Joyce's article offers a more accurate ending to the famous, *"If Mama ain't happy..."* saying. It goes something like this: *"If Mama ain't happy then Mama needs to: Be led by the Spirit; simplify her life; pray with boldness; be quick to forgive; obey God; be herself; and let God invade every area of her life."*

The Problem: I need consistent joy.

The Promise: Being with You will fill me with joy.

The Plan: For a better understanding of God's joy, read Psalm 27:5-7, Psalm 4:6-8, Psalm 21:5-7.

Are You a Priority?

Seek first God's kingdom and what God wants.
Then all your other needs will be met as well.

Mathew 6:33

I was feeling overwhelmed and underappreciated and had called a friend to whine about it. After listening to my grumbles, my friend suggested that I draw a picture of how I viewed my priorities. I wasn't entirely sure how drawing a picture was going to help me, but I trusted my friend and agreed to do so.

Deciding to draw my masterpiece picture of priorities in my Bible, I grabbed a black ball point pen and drew a big bubble cross followed by four stick figures, which represented my husband and my three children. Below the picture I wrote "God" (depicting that He came first), then I wrote "Family, Ministry, Work."

Finishing my masterpiece, I called my friend again and proudly told her of my stick figure drawings and words of priority. I wanted to thank her for the activity suggestion as it was fun to doodle, though I still didn't understand what it had to do with my earlier whining. Before I could say thank you to my friend, she asked a question: "Where are you in your picture?" Bewildered, I looked down at my drawing and suddenly realized I wasn't in it.

If I had been truly seeking God first as my drawing suggested, then I would have understood the importance of the first stick figure after the cross being me. I whined and blamed when what I needed to do was to tend to my relationship with God first in order to set everything else in proper motion.

So tell the truth, can you relate?

The Problem: I'm not appreciated.

The Promise: Seek first God's kingdom and what God wants. Then all your other needs will be met as well.

The Plan: Draw a picture of your priorities. If you're not in the picture, it's time for a new drawing.

A Season for Everything

There is a time for everything.

Ecclesiastes 3:1

As I come to the end of this book that shares many of my hormonal moments between mother and teen daughter, it only seems fitting to end with Ecclesiastes, a book of seasons.

The season of raising solid, God-fearing, hormonally balanced teenage daughters can be challenging, but just as there is a time for that season, a new season will surely come.

God blessed me through my season of scrambled hormones as He taught me to bring my worry, anxiety and fear to Him. Now in this new season my daughters and I are all growing into the women God has created us to be.

The Problem: Some seasons are really tough.

The Promise: There is a time for everything.

The Plan: Meditate on Ecclesiastes 3:1-8.

Scrambled Hormones

There is a time for everything...
and everything on earth has its special season.
There is a time to be born...
and a time to die.
There is a time to plant...
and a time to pull up plants.
There is a time to kill...
and a time to heal.
There is a time to destroy...
and a time to build.
There is a time to cry...
and a time to laugh.
There is a time to be sad...
and a time to dance.
There is a time to throw away stones...
and a time to gather them.
There is a time to hug...
and a time not to hug.
There is a time to look for something...
and a time to stop looking for it.
There is a time to keep things...
and a time to throw things away.
There is a time to tear apart...
and a time to sew together.
There is a time to be silent...
and a time to speak.
There is a time to love...
and a time to hate.
There is a time for war...
and a time for peace.

Mom Testimonies

Quiet Yet Strong-Willed

By Lisa Richardson

My youngest daughter is a quiet, yet strong-willed, young, twenty-year-old. She was always one that wanted to do things her way without help. I was not used to this, as my other two children depended on me quite a bit. I did not know how to deal with such an independent little one. I had to adjust and I did. I did this through prayer.

It wasn't until her father and I divorced that I began to reap the backlash of that strong-willed personality, which I later realized was anger and fear. My now not-so-little daughter began back-talking me and sharply responding to the simplest questions and conversations. I wondered what I had done. The divorce was never brought up by any of my children. In fact, they seemed relieved as the discourse would finally end. Apparently this was not the case when it came to my little warrior.

My days were spent asking her to come out of her room and sit and watch television with me rather than stay secluded in her room. I always received a firm but short, "I'm good." This led me to begin to seek God for the "keys" to get through to my "baby." I prayed and sought advice from friends.

One night as I was reading God's Word, I ran across many scriptures that seemed to scream, "Ask, Seek and Knock!" and "Trust in the Lord. Leaning Not on our Own understanding." I did. I asked night and day. This was a stressful time for me, as I thought I was losing my daughter. The Lord was all I had. I had to trust that He would step in. He did!

Although it took a couple of years, my daughter began to lean on the Lord passionately. She now serves in many ministries, is in leadership, writes sermons, evangelizes and has given her testimony to several unbelievers. Oh, and by the way, she has come to me and apologized for her behavior toward me and why she lashed out the way she did. Our relationship is better than it has ever been. This proves to me that God answers prayers and can and will use those we want to give up on as long as we seek, ask, knock and trust that He is in control.

Praying Through The Teen Years

By Kerry Harris

I can now say, although the youngest is 20 days away from turning 18 years old, that I have successfully raised four daughters and a son, but he was easy.

When my friend Monica asked me to share a brief story of raising my daughter where I experienced God's hand over a certain situation, I had a difficult time coming up with one certain experience. I can honestly say that I would not have survived (and maybe neither would my girls) had it not been for God's grace and provisions throughout those trying teenage, hormonal years. My memories are fading as the years pass by. My first three girls are now 34, 32 and 30. I can remember feeling like I was wearing referee stripes most of the time while the girls were young and fighting over clothes. All I would hear was, "She wore my shirt to school without asking!" I would argue that it is nice to share and why is it that they are ok with sharing with a friend but not their own sister?

I raised the girls in church and I prayed that they would continue to grow in their faith. I hoped I was a good example of right and wrong. I can remember getting that call that a parent dreads, well, one of them anyway…it was the police and I needed to come to a store at the mall immediately. At the time of the call, I was on the couch nursing my youngest. How in the world was I going to get to the store where they were holding my thief while having a 3 week old in tow?

Of course, all of those thoughts were going through my head: Didn't she pay attention while being taught the 10 commandments? Where did I go wrong? How could my daughter do such a thing? What was I going to say to her? What punishment would fit the crime? I was so distraught. My first thought was that she was going to be grounded for life. I was shaking and honestly wasn't sure I could even make the drive to the mall then I remembered to stop and pray.

I can only describe a peace that truly surpasses all understanding by the time I came to the end of my prayer. By the time I saw my daughter face to face, I think even she was surprised by how calm I was. I gave her a grounding that outdid all previous groundings but I believe that the peace she saw me possess, and I later told her came from the Holy Spirit, was a lesson for her also. My daughter realized the errors of her ways and after hearing her side of the story, I believe she succumbed to peer pressure as the friend she was with was apparently a repeat offender. I am happy to say that she never stole again and I know she was impacted by the power of prayer knowing that I would not have had peace that day without it.

God doesn't give us perfect lives with perfect children, but what He does give us is His perfect Love to overcome life's imperfections.

Me, My Daughter and Fear

By Sheryl Griffin

As the mother of a daughter who is now in her mid-twenties, married and hopeful to have children of her own soon, I look back over her teen years with mixed feelings. They say hindsight is always 20/20, and while I can somewhat agree, I also believe getting to the root of the "why's" in your life and being spiritually and emotionally healthy (or at least more so than you were) is much more helpful than hindsight.

I think most mothers have at least one area (if not several) that they have experienced as a teen or young adult that they want to protect their daughter from. But, sometimes without realizing it, we push them to the very situations we want to protect them from.

One area that I wanted desperately to be different for my daughter was premarital sex. My mother, grandmother and I were all sexually active and pregnant by or before the age of fifteen. I had my first abortion at the age of fifteen. While it wasn't wrong of me to want something different for my daughter, the way I went about it unknowingly put pressure and expectations on her to break this particular generational sin.

I thought I had done all the "right" things. I talked openly with her about my mistakes and my past, we encouraged her to take a purity class, we signed contracts stating she would wait until marriage and that she would trust our input on future relationships. We gave her a purity ring. We were involved in church on Sunday mornings and Wednesday nights. I stayed involved with her activities. All the right things...right?

Wrong. I was desperately trying to do God's job (*without realizing it*). Even though all of those things are good, it was my ulterior motive that was not in the right perspective. I was trying to dot every *i* and cross every *t* to ensure she would make different choices. Hoping this would guarantee the outcome I wanted. My desire to protect my daughter from the negative consequences and potential regrets she may have made was not wrong, nor was my openness about my past, the purity class she took or our church involvement. My heart motive was to prepare her and give her all that I felt I lacked growing up, but in doing so I also wanted to wipe away any choice she may have had.

I know now my root issue was fear. I was afraid God would allow my daughter the free will to choose anyway. And the truth of the matter is...He does! My heart motivation was to protect her, but at the cost of fear. This put pressure and expectations on her unfairly. While she chose to oblige our wishes and rules during high school, when she went off to college she began to question everything and found herself in one compromising situation after another. It ended up being a challenging two years before she came forward, confessed, and repented. She wanted accountability, and she was clear in her heart and mind about where she wanted to be and who she was in Christ. But it took time, lots of prayer, and unfortunately, some decisions and experiences of her own that brought her to this place.

It is important to clearly state your expectations, values and family rules, as well as consequences for rebellion or defiance, but you also want to make sure you get to the root of the entire issue. Examine why this is important to you, and help your teen daughter do more than simply go through the motions at the time. Otherwise, it's simply putting a bandage over something that will ultimately require serious attention later on in life.

We need to prepare our daughters and set boundaries, but also recognize that if they choose to go against the expectations we have set, it is a reflection of their heart, and something is going on at a deeper level with them that needs to be dealt with in a proactive way. Just as we have free will to choose, so do our children. The teen years certainly bring different challenges. The ultimate goal is to prepare them to leave the nest, be successful, content, love God and be on track with life.

My Daughter Is Free

By Lisa Richardson

A s a mother of three - two girls and one boy - I had to deal with three different personalities. I knew this but did not know just how different these personalities would be.

My oldest is a girl. She was special to us because she was our first. I did and do adore her! She was my mini-me as well as my shadow. Where I went, she went. When I moved, she moved. We were inseparable. I loved it! However, she became very fearful of many things and people. I prayed continually for the Lord to take her fears away and to cause her to lean on Him.

One night there was a flood in our city. She was so fearful and couldn't sleep. I came to her and prayed over her. I told her about the promise God gave us to never flood and destroy the earth again. I told her to remember that, and when she couldn't sleep to say the name of Jesus over and over again. She developed this habit and applied it in every situation that brought fear to her. To this day she uses my advice and is relieved. My prayers were answered! My daughter is free from most fears, and when she does get fearful, she turns to God...her strength!

Scrambled Hormones

Mom Tips

Navigate Life
With Your Teen Daughter

By Sheryl Griffin
author, A Scarlet Cord of Hope

1. A praying parent is a wise parent. Pray for and with your children daily.

2. Be clear about expectations and consequences.

3. Be willing to dig to the root of difficult issues.

4. Ask questions and be involved. Do not "check out."

5. Be willing to seek guidance or wisdom from moms who have journeyed through the teen season.

6. Recognize this is a short season in life, even though at times, it may seem much longer.

7. Doing all the "right" parenting things does not guarantee your child will always follow through on the expected behavior.

8. Going to church does not make you a Christian anymore than going to a purity class makes you pure. Your teen needs to understand the value of owning it for themselves.

9. Every person must decide at some point in their life what they believe in. Is it their belief/desire or is it only what they were raised to do?

10. Make sure you are living out what you expect your teen to live out.

From Coach Marita
Help for Mom

By Marita A. Cooper
Marriage & Family Therapist

1. Educate yourself spiritually: The Holy Bible has many spiritual principles regarding relationships.

2. Educate yourself on the subject: Explore helpful resources regarding mother/daughter struggles during teen years.

3. Pray with your whole heart: Ask God for guidance and direction through talking and listening prayers.

4. Care for yourself: Connect with at least one positive person who will listen to you without judging.

5 Fellowship with others: Overcome loneliness by socializing with others who will offer support.

6. Get moving and spend time with nature: Join God's creation and exercise to be refreshed and regain your focus.

7. Be a safe person: Surround yourself with trustworthy safe people, as you also are being a safe person for healthy relationships.

10 Ways Working Moms Can Take Care of Themselves

By Jean Johnson
Life Transition Coach

1. Get enough sleep. This means making sure the kids go to bed early enough so you can. Have an evening routine that is calming for everyone.

2. Eat well. Yes, you know it. Most of you don't do it. It is just as easy to grab a piece of fruit as a basket of fries. You and your kids will feel better if you eat three good meals a day. Do the shopping, planning and cooking together. This gives you bonding time and teaches the kids good skills to help out around the house.

3. Exercise. I know you're exhausted at night and don't have time in the morning, but if you're stopping for coffee or vegging out in front of the TV you have time. Do something - anything. It all helps. Better yet - take a class with the kids.

4. Look your best. Get a great haircut. Wear the best clothes you can afford. When we look good we feel good and we smile more.

5. *Smile.* You'll automatically feel better. Even better - laugh.

6. *Count your blessings.* Your mother was right, count your blessings. Make a gratitude list. We all have a multitude of things to be grateful for. Post your list and add to it. Have the kids make one too.

7. *Ask for help.* We don't have to do it all alone. Ask family, friends, co-workers and organizations for help. From babysitting to yard cleanup to a ride to the store, people love to be needed. (Just don't use them.)

8. *Help others.* Nothing feels as good as service. Get the kids involved. Help clean up the beach or mow the elderly neighbor's lawn. Helping each other makes all our lives easier.

9. *Connect to your spirituality.* Whatever that is for you. Nature, music, church, gardening. Do something at least once a week that makes you feel whole.

10. *Lower your expectations.* Yes. *Lower* your expectations of yourself and of your kids. You're not supermom and they aren't super-kids. Cut all of you some slack.

Scrambled Hormones

151

About the Author

Monica Cane is a freelance faith writer from Northern California whose articles have appeared in numerous national print and online publications. She is the author of *A Breath of Inspiration, Fresh Inspiration, The Lost Coin* and *A Journey to Healing: Life after SIDS*, and is a contributing author to the *Cup of Comfort* series from Adams Media.

Married for over 22-years, Monica enjoys spending time with her husband, two grown daughters and their families, along with her teenage son who says he prefers his hormones "sunny-side up, not scrambled."

Connect with Monica:
Facebook: www.facebook.com/MonicaCaneAuthor

Twitter: @Thought_4_2day

Email: ABreathOfInspiration@yahoo.com

Website: www.Abreathofinspiration.com

You might also enjoy these fine books from:

WordCrafts Press

ProVerb Ponderings
    (31 Ruminations on Positive Action)
by Rodney Boyd

Morning Mist
    (Stories from the Water's Edge)
by Barbie Loflin

Why I Failed in the Music Business
    (and how NOT to follow in my footsteps)
by Steve Grossman

Youth Ministry is Easy!
    (and 9 other lies)
by Aaron Shaver

Chronicles of a Believer
by Don McCain

Illuminations
by Paula K. Parker & Tracy Sugg

www.wordcrafts.net

Made in the USA
Middletown, DE
19 January 2018